Test Tube Babies
In-Vitro Fertilization

Ann Fullick

Heinemann Library
Chicago, Illinois

Customer Service 888-454-2279

Visit our website at www.heinemannlibrary.com

Designed by Tinstar Design
Illustrations by Art Construction
Originated by Ambassador Litho Ltd.
Printed and bound in Hong Kong/China

06 05 04 03 02
10 9 8 7 6 5 4 3 2 1

Library of Congress Cataloging-in-Publication Data
Fullick, Ann, 1956-
   Test tube babies : in-vitro fertilization / Ann Fullick.
      p. cm. -- (Science at the edge)
Includes bibliographical references and index.
   ISBN 1-58810-703-5
   1. Fertilization in vitro, Human--Juvenile literature. [1. Test tube
babies. 2. Infertility. 3. Human reproduction.] I. Title. II. Series.
RG135 .F855 2002
618.1'78059--dc21
                                        2001006080

Acknowledgments
The Publisher would like to thank the following for permission to reproduce photographs: pp. 4, 7, 13, 14, 25, 28, 34, 44, 48, 55, 56 Science Photo Library; p. 9 Anna Palmer/Corbis; p. 10 Jonathan Chappell/Bubbles; p. 12 Sally and Richard Greenhill; p. 17 Camera Press; p. 18 Mary Evans Picture Library; p. 21 Dr. Yorgos Nikas/Science Photo Library; p. 22 Rex Features; pp. 23, 43 Popperfoto; p. 26 The Wellcome Trust Photo Library; p. 27 Dan McCoy/Medipics; p. 30 Tudor Photography; pp. 32, 54 PA Photos; p. 33 Michael Dooley; pp. 35, 49 Topham Picturepoint; pp. 36, 41 Doriver Lilley; p. 39 CARE at the Park Hospital; p. 51 Associated Press; p. 53 Scott T. Smith/Corbis; p. 57 Press Association/Topham Picturepoint.

Cover photograph reproduced with permission of Science Photo Library.

Thanks for their invaluable input to Doriver and Ian Lilley, Nicola Monks, Michael Dooley and Pip Scorey.

Some words are shown in bold, **like this.** You can find out what they mean by looking in the glossary.

Contents

An Everyday Miracle? 4

What Causes Infertility? 10

Treating Infertility without IVF 16

The IVF Story 18

How Does IVF Work? 24

The Price of Success 32

Doriver's Story 36

Beyond IVF 42

Ethics, Issues, and the Law 46

Where Do We Go from Here? 54

Timeline 58

Glossary *60*

Further Reading *63*

Index *64*

An Everyday Miracle?

Every moment of every day a baby is born somewhere around the world. Each new human being is born as the result of the joining of two tiny cells from the parents to form a single new cell. It is this cell that then grows and divides to form the billions of cells that make up the body of a newborn baby.

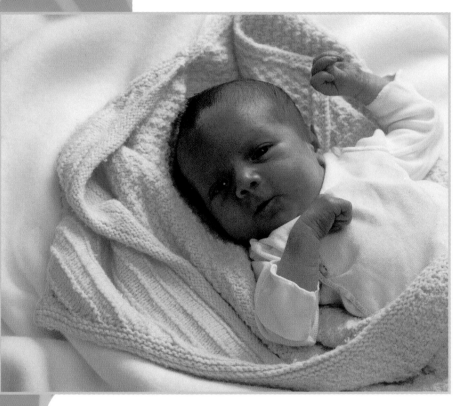

It happens every day, but the safe arrival of a baby that has grown over the course of nine months from a single fertilized human egg cell is still an amazing event.

Infertility

For lots of people, having babies is very easy. There is a time each month when, if the couple has sexual intercourse, there is a chance that an **ovum** (egg) in the woman's body will be **fertilized** by a **sperm** from the man. Nine months later a new baby will be born. In fact, many people spend years trying to avoid pregnancy, using different methods of **contraception** to make sure that sperm and eggs don't meet. But what happens if pregnancy and babies don't happen when they *are* wanted?

Infertility has always been an issue. Back in the 1500s King Henry VIII of England got rid of several wives who could not give birth to the son and heir he so desperately wanted! The lives of many ordinary people have also been saddened by the inability to have a much-wanted child. Although there are many different causes of infertility, for centuries the solutions were few. The main options were adopting a child or trying to accept the idea of childlessness.

> *Not being able to have a baby of your own is the most heart-breaking experience.*
>
> Jilly Cooper, journalist and writer

So what can we do about it today? In the past 50 years, it has become increasingly possible to treat and overcome at least some forms of infertility. A wide variety of options are now available for couples who cannot have a child naturally. These range from simple tests that make it possible to pinpoint when a woman is most likely to get pregnant to complex techniques such as **in vitro fertilization,** or IVF. This is a process in which an egg and sperm are brought together outside the mother's body. They are usually mixed in a glass **Petri dish**, hence the name in vitro fertilization. In vitro is Latin for "in glass." The developing **embryo** is then replaced in the mother's body. The development of IVF has resulted in the births of thousands of babies around the world to people who would otherwise have had no hope of becoming pregnant. And IVF has led the way for the development of other methods to help couples have babies. These even include injecting a single sperm into an egg before replacing it in the mother's body.

Like most scientific breakthroughs, our increased ability to control human **fertility** is something of a mixed blessing. It can bring great happiness to couples who would otherwise be unable to have a child. At the same time it also raises many questions about embryos that are created and then not needed. In addition, it introduces the possibility of changing the inherited material of an embryo before it is returned to the mother. As more sophisticated treatments for infertility are discovered, the **ethics** of each need to be discussed. Yet the driving force behind the whole technology remains the strong desire of infertile couples to have a child of their own.

The biology of reproduction

Young children cannot have children of their own. However, as they grow and mature the parts of the body involved in **reproduction** become active. These parts of the body include the sexual organs and the **pituitary gland** in the brain. For many people these systems start up and run fairly smoothly. But for a growing number, things do not quite work as they should. So how does the body of a healthy, fertile woman or man work?

The fertile female

For about two days in every month a woman is fertile. She has produced an egg that is mature and ready to meet a **sperm.** The events leading up to and following this special time form a 28-day cycle of **fertility,** called the **menstrual cycle.**

Inside the body of every newborn baby girl are the eggs (called ova) that may form her future children. Once the girl goes through **puberty,** the **ovaries,** which contain the eggs, become active in response to chemical signals called **hormones.**

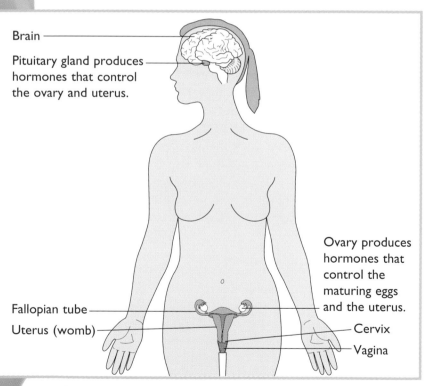

Brain

Pituitary gland produces hormones that control the ovary and uterus.

Ovary produces hormones that control the maturing eggs and the uterus.

Fallopian tube

Uterus (womb)

Cervix

Vagina

A delicate balance of hormones controls the reproductive system in a woman.

Follicle Stimulating Hormone (FSH) is made by the pituitary gland in the brain. FSH has a direct effect on the ovaries. It makes some of the eggs grow and mature, ready for release. FSH also makes the ovary produce another female hormone, **estrogen**. This triggers the buildup of the lining of the **uterus** (the organ in which the baby grows and develops) so it will be ready to nurture a pregnancy. After about fourteen days an egg is released. This is known as **ovulation**. The egg then leaves the ovary. The egg travels through the **fallopian tube** toward the uterus. If it meets some sperm on the way up, it may be **fertilized** and a pregnancy will begin. If not, the lining of the uterus breaks down and passes out of the body. This is called menstruation.

Reproduction in the male

Men do not have a reproductive cycle as women do, but they do have male reproductive hormones produced by the pituitary gland and by the male sex organs, the **testes**. In response to these hormones the testes make a constant supply of sperm. Other glands make the various secretions that are mixed with the sperm to form **semen**.

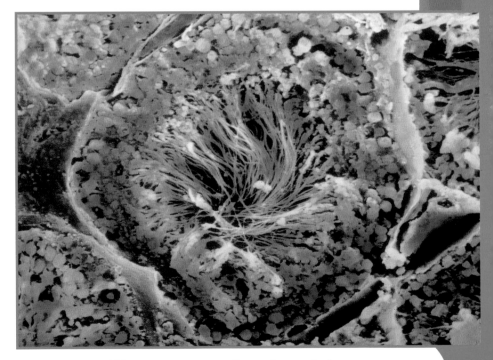

Whereas women usually produce a single mature egg each month, millions of sperm are produced all the time in the testes. The tails of hundreds of developing sperm can be seen here, in a tiny tube in the testes.

From conception to birth

Once a couple decides they want a baby they need to try and make sure that **sperm** are present when a mature egg is released from the woman's **ovary.** Every time they have sex the man releases **semen** containing millions of sperm into the woman's vagina. If the woman is at the fertile point in her **menstrual cycle,** an egg will be released from the ovary and begin its journey along the **fallopian tube.** How do the egg and the sperm meet?

The egg cannot move on its own. It is helped along the fallopian tube by the beating of millions of tiny hairlike cilia. The cilia move it slowly away from the ovary toward the **uterus.** After **ovulation** the egg lives only for about 48 hours.

The sperm, on the other hand, have an enormously long journey to make as they travel through **mucus** and other secretions in the vagina and **cervix,** up through the uterus, and on into the fallopian tube that contains the egg. The journey of a single sperm can be compared to a person setting off from New York and swimming across the Atlantic Ocean to England!

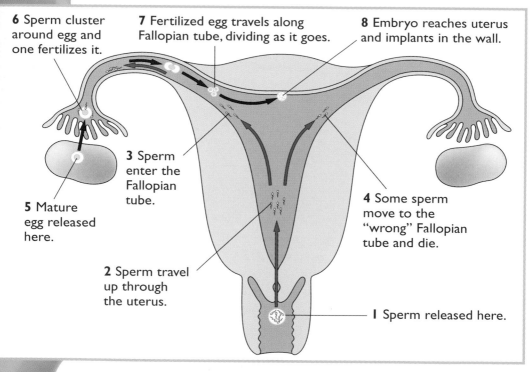

6 Sperm cluster around egg and one fertilizes it.

7 Fertilized egg travels along Fallopian tube, dividing as it goes.

8 Embryo reaches uterus and implants in the wall.

3 Sperm enter the Fallopian tube.

5 Mature egg released here.

4 Some sperm move to the "wrong" Fallopian tube and die.

2 Sperm travel up through the uterus.

1 Sperm released here.

The fallopian tubes are the site where the egg and the sperm meet at **fertilization** and where the first divisions of the newly formed **embryo** take place.

Each sperm makes lashing movements with its tail that keep it suspended in the liquids. It is moved toward the egg by natural muscle movements of the uterus. Some sperm reach the fallopian tubes very quickly—in a matter of minutes—but millions never reach the tubes. This is why so many sperm are produced in the first place, because the odds against any of them reaching the egg are so high!

Fertilization

Once the sperm reach the egg, how is the egg actually fertilized? The sperm cluster around the egg, attracted by chemical messages the egg sends out. Special digestive **enzymes** in the head of the sperm act to dissolve away the protective jelly coating of the egg. Finally one sperm manages to break through and get inside the egg. After this happens, no other sperm can get in. The **nucleus** of the sperm contains **genetic** information from the man, while the nucleus of the egg contains genetic information from the woman. Once they fuse together, fertilization has taken place, a new genetic individual is formed, and a potential new life has begun.

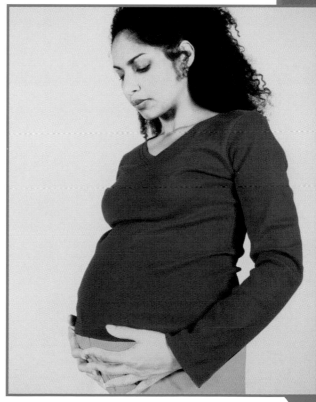

After fertilization, the single cell begins to grow and divide as it continues to travel along the fallopian tube to the uterus. By the time it reaches the uterus, it is a small ball of cells ready to implant itself in the blood-rich lining that has developed in order to support it.

Once the fertilized egg has implanted itself in the uterus, cell divisions, the specialization of tissue, and lots of growth take place. After nine months, a fully formed baby human being is ready to be born and take a place in the world.

What Causes Infertility?

When a couple decides that they want to begin to try to have a baby, most expect to get pregnant right away. After all, many of them have spent years trying very hard not to get pregnant by mistake! However, even if a young, **fertile** couple have sexual intercourse at the right stage of the monthly cycle there is no guarantee that they will become pregnant. The chance that they will conceive gets steadily lower as they get older, and it is also reduced by lifestyle factors such as smoking, drinking, and being overweight.

For an increasing number of couples, the months without a positive pregnancy test turn into years. When **infertility** seems to be staring people in the face, it becomes very important to understand why pregnancy is not happening and what, if anything, can be done about it.

When pregnancy doesn't happen, even children's clothes in a shop window can make it seem as if everyone else has a baby.

Whose problem?

Often, if a couple cannot have a child, they wonder whose "fault" it is. For centuries it was assumed that childlessness was the fault of the woman. We now know better. Failing to get pregnant can be the result of problems in the man, the woman, or even in both partners.

In about a third of all cases of infertility there is indeed a problem in the way that the body of the woman is working. However, in more than a third of the cases, it is the reproductive system of the man that is not functioning as it should. The final group of infertility cases are either the result of both the man and the woman being a bit less fertile than normal or—the most puzzling of all—both partners seem to be healthy but pregnancy just doesn't happen.

Finding out

IVF has been successful in helping to overcome some forms of infertility, but it is still a very specialized area of medicine. A couple that is having problems in conceiving a baby does not start the quest for a child with the IVF specialist. They begin with the family doctor.

Typically a doctor will check the general health of the couple in case there are any other causes of infertility not related to their reproductive systems. The doctor will also check whether the couple are having sexual intercourse when the woman is most fertile. The doctor will also ask about any other medicines either partner may be taking and whether either of them smokes or drinks alcohol. Sometimes this allows the doctor to find a simple solution to fertility problems so that further medical treatment is not needed.

For many the solution is not quite so simple. A doctor will usually refer a couple to an infertility specialist when it becomes clear that they are having real difficulty in conceiving. For older couples, especially, the "biological clock" is ticking. A woman's fertility begins to fall as she approaches 40. It is important that they start working with an infertility specialist as soon as possible. Most specialists would rather see couples with fertility problems sooner rather than later in order to best help them find a successful solution to their problems.

An infertile woman

When a couple can't have a baby, a number of different tests are carried out on both partners to try and find out the cause of the **infertility**. Different causes call for different solutions.

Ovulation problems

To find out why a woman is not conceiving, doctors look for both physical and chemical causes. One of the first checks will be to see if **ovulation** is occurring. No egg equals no baby!

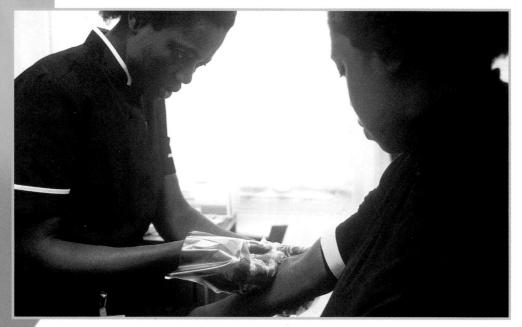

By measuring the levels of different **hormones** in the blood, doctors can get a good idea of what is going on and whether ovulation is taking place.

It is estimated that problems with ovulation occur in 25 percent of infertile couples. This is an important problem to identify, as most of these patients can be treated successfully.
  Susan Smith, Deputy Medical Director, Bridge Fertility Centre, Britain

There can be several explanations for a lack of ovulation. Sometimes there are no eggs in the **ovaries**. However, this is relatively rare and is the cause of infertility in only one to two percent of the women who have difficulty in conceiving. If there are no eggs, then the woman will never conceive naturally. IVF can help provide her only chance of motherhood. Some women who have had families of their own are prepared to act as egg **donors.** This means they allow eggs to be collected from their ovaries and given to other, infertile women. A donated egg can be **fertilized** by **sperm** from the infertile woman's partner and placed in her body to develop.

However, in many women who do not ovulate the cause is easier to deal with. Some women don't make enough **FSH** to stimulate the release of the mature eggs from the ovary and others don't make any at all. Synthetic (laboratory-created) hormones can be used that will replace natural FSH, bringing about ovulation and so, hopefully, pregnancy.

Tangled tubes?

The most common female physical problem preventing pregnancy is that the **fallopian tubes** are twisted, scarred, or blocked in some way. The fallopian tubes are inside the body, hidden to human eyes. About 4.3 inches (11 centimeters) long, they lead from the ovaries to the **uterus.** If the tubes are damaged, this prevents the sperm from meeting the egg. Damaged tubes will also stop the egg, fertilized or not, from traveling along to the uterus. Thirty percent of female infertility is the result of damaged fallopian tubes.

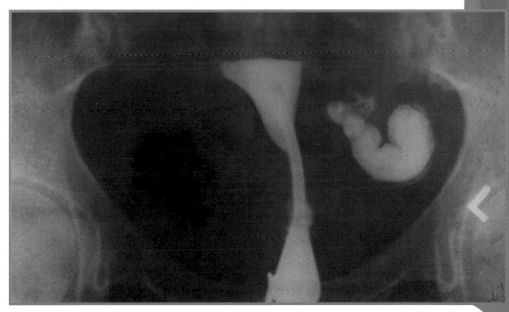

A test called a hysterosalpingogram helps doctors find out if the uterus is normally shaped and if the fallopian tubes are open. If the fallopian tubes are damaged, as these are, a normal **conception** is impossible. In this picture, the uterus is the pale, triangular shape in the center. The fallopian tube on the left of the picture is not visible, which indicates to doctors that it is blocked. The tube on the right is damaged.

Damage to the tubes is revealed during a procedure known as a **laparoscopy**. During a laparoscopy a very small telescope is inserted into the abdominal cavity so doctors can look at the **fallopian tubes** from the outside. The woman is given a general anesthetic so that she is unconscious during this procedure. Next, a special dye is injected through the **cervix,** and the doctors watch to see how the dye moves through the fallopian tubes. If the tubes are not blocked, the dye will spill out of the ends of the tubes. These tests give a good first idea of whether or not the tubes are blocked or if there are any abnormalities in the **uterus** itself. If there seem to be problems, the investigation can be taken further with a hysterosalpingogram. For this a special dye that shows up on X-rays is injected up into the cervix. X-rays are then taken, and the dye reveals in the X-rays any blockages in the fallopian tubes.

Sometimes doctors will insert special instruments into blocked fallopian tubes to try to reopen them. This technique, however, can damage the very delicate tubes. When the tubes are badly damaged or blocked, then the only possible solution is IVF.

An infertile man

When a couple visits a doctor about **fertility** problems, investigations will be made into the fertility of the man as well as the woman. There are two crucial factors. Is the man producing **sperm** in his **semen**, and are they normal, healthy, and active? The answer to both of these questions comes from a careful examination of the man's semen.

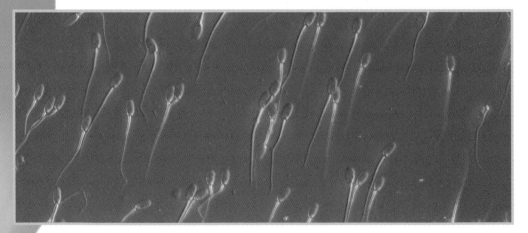

Using a microscope to view a fresh sample of semen reveals the health of the sperm and shows how many are present.

In normal healthy semen there will be hundreds of millions of sperm. In fact, the lowest number of sperm counted as normal is 20 million sperm per milliliter (one milliliter = 0.03 ounce) of semen! Once the sperm count falls below this level it begins to affect fertility. Remember, only one out of every 2,000 sperm will make it from the cervix to the fallopian tubes. If the sperm count is just a bit below normal, there are certain things that the man can do to increase the numbers. If the **testes** get too warm, the level of sperm production falls, so taking cool showers and wearing loose-fitting underwear and clothing can help to increase the sperm count. Smoking and drinking alcohol are known to lower the sperm count as well, so reducing or stopping these habits can also help increase sperm numbers. If the count is very low, however, the problem is more difficult.

Numbers aren't everything

Sperm count is important, but the ability of sperm to fertilize eggs successfully depends on more than numbers. The sperm's ability to move, or motility, is very important, too. In other words, how active are the sperm and how well do they swim? For the man to be fertile his sperm need to have actively lashing tails. Around half of them must swim forward in straight lines rather than around and around in circles.

Even if a man has lots of active sperm, that may not be enough to be sure that he is fertile. It is also very important that the semen doesn't contain too many abnormal sperm. Every man produces a certain number of sperm with two heads instead of one, or with two tails, or with broken necks. But if the percentage of these abnormal sperm gets too high, then the chances of a successful pregnancy fall.

Overcoming male **infertility** is not easy. Until recently the best hope was for the woman to be treated with healthy sperm given by an unknown **donor**, often mixed with some of her partner's sperm. However, some of the latest developments of IVF involve using a single normal sperm and injecting it into the woman's egg cell, which is then implanted in her uterus. This new development is leading to potential treatment for almost all men with fertility problems, because the number of men who produce no healthy sperm at all is relatively small.

There are very few cases of male infertility or subfertility that can actually be cured. Generally when we refer to treatment we mean techniques that enable us to ***circumvent*** *the problem.*
> Sue Avery, Scientific Director, Bourn Hall Clinic, Britain

Treating Infertility without IVF

The best-known treatment for **infertility** is, without a doubt, IVF. The IVF procedure is often in the news, because of the many new treatments that have come about in the years following its introduction. But when a couple first has **fertility** problems, their treatment will not always involve IVF.

Smoking, drinking alcohol, being very overweight or underweight, eating an unhealthy diet, or having a lack of folic acid (a type of B vitamin) in the diet can make it difficult or impossible to conceive. For a surprising number of people, simple changes in lifestyle can make **conception** possible and result in the birth of a baby.

> *Without very overweight or very underweight patients—in other words, if everyone was within the ideal weight range—the number of patients in my infertility clinic would be significantly reduced.*
>
> Michael Dooley, Consultant,
> Winterbourne Hospital Infertility Clinic, Britain

One of the most common ways of treating fertility problems involves **fertility drugs**. These are not only remarkably successful in their own right, but have also paved the way for the development of IVF. One of the main reasons women fail to get pregnant is that they do not produce mature eggs. Fertility drugs are chemicals that work in different ways to stimulate the woman's body to produce and release a mature egg from the **ovary**.

The most widely used fertility drug is clomiphene citrate. This drug works by getting the body to make extra **FSH** to stimulate the production of eggs by the ovaries. When women do not make any of their own FSH they can be given different drugs that actually contain human **hormones**. These stimulate the ovaries directly. Other fertility drugs can be used if the mature eggs are not released from the ovaries.

The use of these drugs has been very successful in helping many infertile couples have children, and it has been key to the development of IVF. To carry out IVF, doctors need to harvest a number of eggs to **fertilize** outside the body. Even with fertile women, only one or at most two eggs mature enough each month to be released from the ovary. So when doctors are working with their patients toward IVF, fertility drugs are an important part of the preparation.

Three's a crowd?

Fertility drugs have helped many infertile couples have children, but when the drugs were first developed they caused problems of their own. In the early days of fertility drugs, doctors were not always sure of the doses to use, and many of the women using the drugs had multiple pregnancies. In other words, more than one egg was released and fertilized at the same time. Twins did not cause too many problems, but far more people than expected had triplets, quadruplets, or even more babies.

Large multiple pregnancies cause many problems. When lots of babies develop in the same **uterus**, there is a much higher risk that labor will start very early because the uterus becomes overstretched. Babies born early are very tiny and are more likely to die or become brain damaged. Now, with increased knowledge of the way fertility drugs work and close control of the dosage, large multiple pregnancies can usually be avoided.

It is reasonable to suppose that a couple eager for a baby would welcome an instant family of three, four, or more children, but it is not quite that simple. If several babies arrive at once, the demands on the parents—physically, mentally, and financially—can be enormous.

The IVF Story

For centuries people have tried to overcome **infertility** by whatever means they had available. Scientists and doctors have worked long and hard to reach the stage we are at today. IVF and other treatments offer the hope of a baby to many who would otherwise be childless. Many aspects of human **fertility** had to be understood before it became possible to **fertilize** a human egg outside of the mother's body and return it to her **uterus** to grow into a full-term, healthy baby.

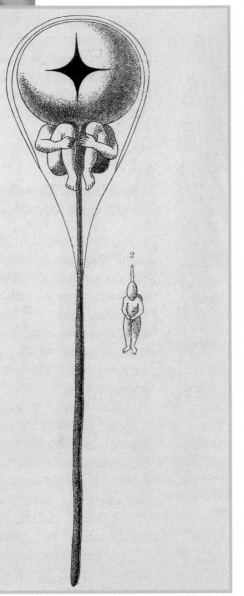

Exploring ways of treating infertility is not a new science. In the 3rd century, Jewish thinkers discussed whether it was possible for women to become pregnant by accidental **artificial insemination.** By the fourteenth century, Arabs were using artificial insemination to breed horses. In 1777 an Italian priest began experiments with artificial insemination

For many years people had little understanding of how human **reproduction** worked. One long-held belief was that the man supplied the entire new baby in his **sperm,** and the woman simply served as a vessel, providing the growing child with all that it needed until it was born. Until beliefs like this were proved wrong by scientific knowledge, any attempts to overcome infertility were doomed to failure.

in reptiles. In 1785 there was a major breakthrough when John Hunter, a Scottish surgeon, first attempted human artificial insemination. As a result of his experiments, a child was born that same year.

Into the 20th century

The 20th century saw many important advances in the treatment of infertility. In the early years of the century, American scientists Samuel Crowe, Harvey Cushing, and John Homans began to unravel the complex chemical control of human fertility. They (along with other scientists) discovered, isolated, and identified the **hormones** made by the **pituitary gland** in the brain and by the **ovaries** and **testes**.

Toward the end of the 20th century there was a great deal of controversy and debate about IVF and some of the other treatments that have developed from it. However, this sort of debate is nothing new. Assisting couples to have babies using artificial means has always raised strong feelings. Even in the early days there were people who were unhappy with what they saw as unnatural tampering with nature.

When early reports of artificial insemination using sperm from a **donor** were published in the *British Medical Journal* in 1945, there was great debate in the British Parliament. At that time British researchers were the leaders in the field. In 1948, the Archbishop of Canterbury, the most senior clergyman in Britain, recommended that the practice should be made a criminal offense. The British government didn't follow that recommendation, although they did say that the practice was "undesirable and not to be encouraged."

The first human **fertility drug** was produced in 1949. However, it was not until 1962 that the first baby was born as a result of drug-triggered **ovulation**. By 1954 there was a report of four successful pregnancies following the use of frozen sperm. By the mid-1970s artificial insemination using donor sperm had become widespread in the U.S., Europe, and Australia. In the U.S. the National Conference of Commissioners on Uniform Laws passed the Uniform Parentage Act (1973), which established that if a married couple under the care of a doctor agrees to undergo artificial insemination with donor sperm, then the husband is considered the natural father of the child that is born. Nineteen states adopted the act, which was revised in 2000.

Understanding grows

As the 1960s dawned, doctors and scientists all over the world were learning more and more about different parts of the process of **reproduction.** All of this knowledge and understanding was needed before IVF could be developed.

Their knowledge included the use of **fertility drugs** to regulate the numbers of eggs that matured in the **ovary.** Developments in the understanding of the ways in which eggs mature and the events of **ovulation** were also important. As scientists moved closer to IVF, it became vitally important that the process of **fertilization** was thoroughly understood. Just as vital was knowledge about the way early human **embryos** develop outside of their natural environment in the body of the mother. It soon became clear that human embryos could not survive long outside the ideal environment of the mother, and so transfer back to the mother would need to be done within the first few days of fertilization.

Only once all of this knowledge and understanding was in place could scientists take the next steps forward and move toward developing IVF.

The early development of the human embryo

How does an embryo develop? Once an egg and a **sperm** have joined, the two **nuclei** fuse together. This means that the **genetic** material of the father combines with the genetic material of the mother. Once this has happened a new cell with a unique combination of **DNA** has formed. The cell begins to divide, and about 30 hours after fertilization the developing embryo has two cells. After 40–50 hours, each of these two cells also has divided in two and the embryo consists of four cells. In the human body, these divisions take place as the fertilized egg is beginning to move down the **fallopian tube.** Cell divisions continue, until there are sixteen cells. About four to five days after fertilization, a hollow ball of about 80 cells arrives in the **uterus,** where it implants itself. At this stage the embryo is called a **blastocyst.** The developing embryo in IVF may be returned to the body of the mother at any stage, from two cells to blastocyst. From then on, the remaining stages of development will take place in the protected environment of her uterus.

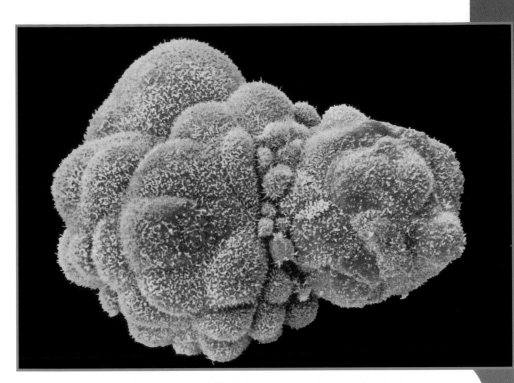

Increasingly, IVF clinics are returning the developing embryo to the uterus at the blastocyst stage rather than at an earlier stage, because this is the point that the embryo would naturally arrive in the uterus and implant.

Edwards and Steptoe

The first time a human egg was fertilized successfully outside of the female body was in 1969. It was achieved by Dr. Robert Edwards, a **physiologist** working at Cambridge University in England. He used human ovaries that had been removed during surgery as the source of the eggs. The eggs needed to be kept in a very special, chemically balanced fluid. They couldn't just be taken out of the body and left in a dish. This first human **in vitro fertilization** took place in a culture medium, which is a mixture of chemicals and water used to help eggs and developing embryos grow. This had been used very successfully for the in vitro fertilization of hamster eggs during earlier, animal-based research into **infertility** treatments.

At the same time, Patrick Steptoe, a **gynecologist** at the Royal Oldham Hospital in Britain, was developing ways of removing mature human eggs from the ovary by **laparoscopy**. He "harvested" eggs by sucking them up from the ripe **follicle** (cell surrounding the egg) at the stage when they could be fertilized. This was quite daring, because at that time laparoscopy was considered a dangerous procedure.

The birth of IVF and Louise Brown

By 1971, Edwards and Steptoe had met and were sharing their ideas to work toward a successful **infertility** treatment. They worked on retrieving eggs from volunteers so they could find out the best time to collect eggs. They also worked on determining the best culture conditions for maintaining a human egg and an early **embryo** outside the body, that is, in vitro. They did not use **fertility drugs** to enhance egg development. They simply monitored their patients very carefully. When **ovulation** appeared about to happen they collected the egg by **laparoscopy**.

Before long they felt ready to attempt a pregnancy in an infertile volunteer. By 1975, success was on the horizon. A human embryo was replaced successfully in its mother's body and a pregnancy began. But the excitement was short-lived. The pregnancy developed not in the **uterus** of the mother but in her **fallopian tube**. This is known as an **ectopic pregnancy**, and it can cause terrible pain and the risk of severe damage or even death to the mother. An operation was carried out to remove the tube, and the embryo with it, crushing the hopes of both doctors and scientists. It was, of course, also a terrible blow for the couple who so wanted a child that they were prepared to act as human guinea pigs in this amazing experiment.

Robert Edwards (on the left) and Patrick Steptoe were the pioneers whose work resulted in the birth of the first IVF baby and gave hope to countless infertile couples.

However, for Edwards and Steptoe success was not far away. They continued their experiments, in spite of growing pressure from the media and from groups who opposed their work as interference with the natural process of **reproduction**. In 1977, the two men removed a single mature egg from the **ovary** of Lesley Brown and fertilized it with **sperm** from her husband. The embryo that resulted was implanted back into Lesley's uterus and she became pregnant. Finally, on July 25, 1978, Louise Brown, a healthy baby girl who had been conceived in a glass **Petri dish** was born. This was truly groundbreaking science. It was also the end of years of heartache for the Browns. Both Steptoe and Edwards were present at the birth. They must have been almost as happy as the Browns! IVF as a way of overcoming infertility had arrived at last.

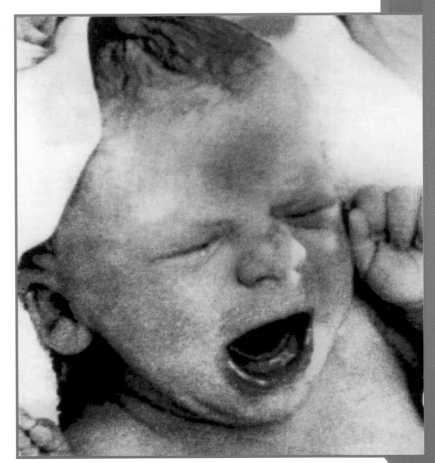

Louise Brown, the first baby born as a result of fertilization outside the body. The media coined the phrase "test-tube baby" to describe her astonishing **conception**, and this term for IVF stuck.

How Does IVF Work?

The birth of Louise Brown in 1978 was the climax of years of research. But it was just the beginning of new **infertility** treatments. In the years since then IVF has continued to develop in a spectacular fashion. The techniques have been refined and new treatments added. Within two years, two Australian groups of researchers helped couples have babies through IVF, but they used a different technique. They treated their patients with **fertility drugs** to make sure that plenty of eggs were produced. Because they had a higher success rate than the British team, it was their methods of egg collection that were widely adopted. Even Edwards and Steptoe later adopted the use of fertility drugs to stimulate the production of more than one egg, a process known as **superovulation**.

IVF offers a way of overcoming infertility for women whose **fallopian tubes** are blocked, twisted, or damaged beyond repair, so that neither eggs nor **sperm** can travel along the tubes. The treatment combines the egg and sperm outside the body and returns the developing **embryo** to the **uterus**, bypassing the need for the fallopian tubes.

If a couple who is infertile because of damaged fallopian tubes decides, in consultation with their doctors, that a course of IVF treatment is the choice for them, what can they expect?

Getting started

Almost every couple who undergoes IVF treatment receives counseling first. This is to make sure that they realize that although the treatment offers them the hope of a baby, it in no way guarantees one. The chances of such a couple actually achieving a successful pregnancy are no higher, and probably lower, than a **fertile** couple attempting to get pregnant by natural methods. If they do get pregnant using IVF, then the risk of multiple pregnancy is higher than for a normal couple. Most clinics feel it is very important that their patients realize these facts before they start treatment.

Infertility clinics, such as this one in Milan, Italy, need to find out as much as they can about their patients as quickly as possible. They use medical notes from the doctors who have carried out earlier investigations into the couple's fertility problem. They also need to talk to the couple to find out what they are looking for and if they are likely to be suitable for the treatments available.

IVF clinics vary widely in who they will accept into their programs. Couples who seek help are not just those with blocked or damaged fallopian tubes. Some couples don't get pregnant and there is no clear reason why not. If they have tried all other methods and failed, IVF may offer them a final chance.

Some clinics will only accept younger couples who are more likely to succeed. They follow this policy to avoid giving false hope to other couples and to keep their "baby per treatment" average as high as possible. The rate of live babies achieved per treatment is one of the most important factors couples look at when deciding which infertility clinic to choose. On the other hand some clinics specialize in the most-difficult-to-treat cases, such as older couples, couples where both partners have infertility problems, and couples who have already had a number of IVF failures.

Paying for the treatments is another issue couples must consider. In the U.S. many health care plans will pay only for limited treatment for infertility. Some will not cover it at all. Couples need to be sure they understand exactly what kind of coverage for infertility their insurance plan offers before starting treatment. They should also check their financial situation if they decide to go ahead with treatments or procedures not covered by their health plans. They will have to pay for any procedures not covered by their health insurance. These treatments can cost thousands of dollars.

Managing IVF

The first important stage of IVF treatment is to make sure that the woman produces a number of good-quality eggs. This is brought about by carefully measured doses of **fertility drugs.** The development of ripe **follicles** on the surface of the **ovary** is then monitored. If not many follicles are developing, doctors will not try to collect eggs. Instead they will try again during the next **menstrual cycle**, giving the woman a higher dosage of drugs.

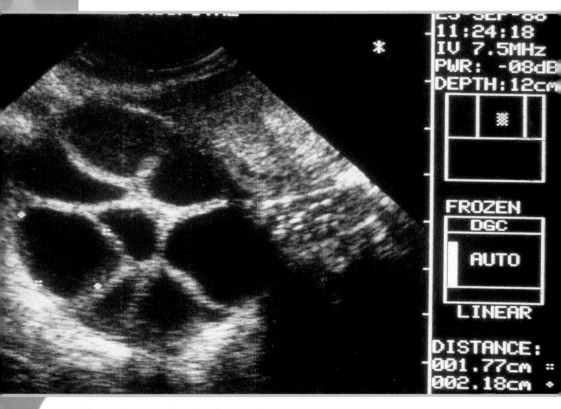

Using ultrasound technology, a doctor can monitor the state of the follicles on the surface of a woman's ovaries without opening up her body.

The development of the eggs maturing in the ovaries is monitored using **ultrasound**, which lets doctors see how many follicles are forming. Blood tests may also be used to monitor levels of a **hormone** called estradiol. As the follicles develop, the levels of estradiol increase. By combining the information from the blood tests and the ultrasound, doctors can build up a very accurate picture of how many eggs are developing in the ovary and when will be the best time to collect them. About 36 hours before the egg collection is due, the woman is given a final injection of yet another hormone, human chorionic gonadotrophin (HCG). This hormone helps make sure that the eggs are fully mature in their follicles.

Collecting the eggs is another key stage of the process. If a number of healthy, mature eggs are not collected, the process cannot go ahead. The presence of ripe follicles in the ovaries does not necessarily mean the eggs will be collected successfully. Harvesting eggs is a tricky and delicate business.

The process is carried out with the woman either sedated or under a general anesthetic. An ultrasound probe is placed inside her vagina. This gives a better picture of the position of the ripe follicles than a probe on the stomach. A needle is carefully guided through the wall of the vagina into the body cavity next to the ovaries. The point is then carefully maneuvered into a ripe follicle. The liquid inside the follicle, including the mature egg, is sucked up into a tube connected to a small pot that collects the harvested eggs.

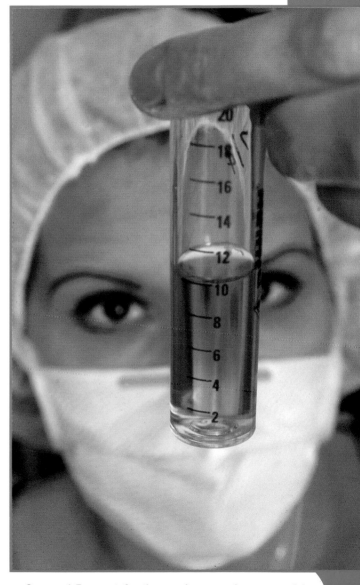

Success! For an infertile couple, even the successful collection of a number of mature eggs is a big step forward. The eggs are held here in a special liquid.

The big moment

Once the eggs have been collected from the woman they are placed in a special liquid similar to normal body fluids. Each egg is put in a small dish in an incubator and kept at body temperature. The acidity level (pH) is also kept the same as the normal body fluids. This is important so that the eggs continue to develop properly. The male partner then produces some **semen**, from which samples of very active **sperm** are taken. About four to six hours after the eggs are collected, the sperm are added to the dishes containing the eggs. The timing matches when they would naturally have been released from the **ovary.** If all goes well with the insemination, the process of **fertilization** begins. This takes about eighteen hours from start to finish. After twelve more hours the first cell division takes place. At this stage a couple finds out if they have actually achieved any **embryos.**

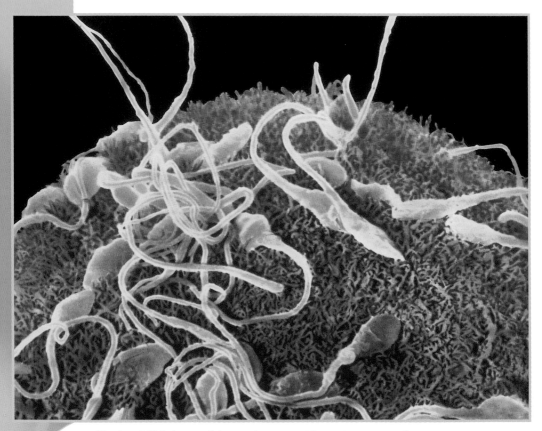

During IVF it is possible to observe with a microscope the process of fertilization. Normally, the process takes place within the **fallopian tubes** and, therefore, can't be observed. This access to the very early embryo means it can be checked for **genetic** defects before it is replaced in the mother's body.

The dividing of these embryonic cells continues for several days. After two days they contain four cells, after three days there are eight cells, and after five days the embryo is a hollow ball of cells called a **blastocyst**. The embryos can be transferred to the woman's body at any of these stages. During this time the health of the tiny embryos will be watched closely by the **embryologist**. The embryologist must be very careful that only healthy, undamaged embryos are replaced in the mother's body. For this reason, the dividing cells are regularly observed through a microscope.

We choose which embryos to replace by looking at their appearance. A good embryo has even cell divisions and the cells aren't forming small fragments. We have a grading system, and the best grades of embryo give the best pregnancy rates. Having said that, we sometimes have embryos with a poor appearance giving rise to healthy pregnancies and equally some beautiful embryos which don't result in pregnancy at all.

Nicola Monk, embryologist,
Winterbourne Hospital Infertility Clinic

Embryo Transfer

In some ways transferring the embryos to the mother's body is the simplest part of the procedure. The hormonal state of the woman's body a few days after **ovulation** means she is ready to receive an embryo. Some embryos, usually two or three, are placed in a very slender tube called a catheter, which is passed up through the woman's **cervix** to the top of the **uterus.** This is the normal and ideal site for the embryo to implant. The tiny balls of cells are deposited here in the uterus. To help improve the chances of pregnancy occurring, many women are given additional treatment with the **hormone progesterone** after the embryos have been replaced.

At this stage the woman can go home and carry on with her ordinary life. It must be very tempting to simply stay in bed and not move, to try and make sure that the tiny embryos stay where they are meant to be! However, all the research shows that this doesn't make the slightest difference as to whether the embryos implant or not. After all, an embryo normally manages to implant no matter what is going on in its mother's life.

Finding out

For an infertile couple, the two weeks immediately following **embryo** transfer must seem endless. They have to wait until the woman would be due to have a **period** before they find out if she is pregnant or not. Of course, if her period starts, then the IVF obviously has not worked. But if the monthly bleeding does not start on the day it is expected then a very sensitive early pregnancy test can show what is happening to the **hormones** in the body. This can indicate whether or not the woman is pregnant.

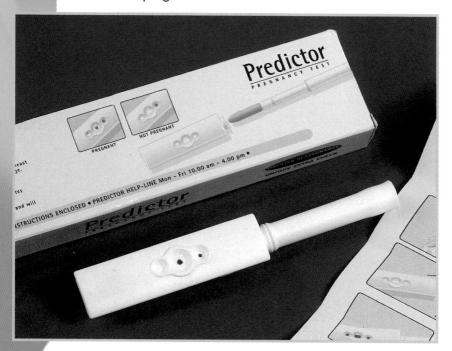

This is the sight that everyone on an IVF program longs to see. A positive pregnancy test means at least one embryo has implanted and a pregnancy has begun.

An **ultrasound** scan carried out four to six weeks after the embryos are transferred will confirm the successful pregnancy and also give the couple their first glimpse of their longed-for child or children. This scan provides important information for the IVF team. It shows them if they have definitely been successful and how many babies are expected. It is also enormously important for the couple concerned, who may well find it very hard to accept the fact that they really are pregnant after trying for so long. Seeing a tiny blob, or blobs, on the ultrasound screen and the beating of a tiny heart definitely helps make the situation seem more real.

Once an IVF pregnancy has been established, it becomes just like any other pregnancy. The worries and fears that every mother has for her unborn child may well be greater in a couple who has tried for years to become pregnant. However, the actual risks are no higher, unless they are expecting twins or triplets. Even then, the risk of problems developing in the pregnancy is no worse than for anyone else expecting more than one baby to arrive.

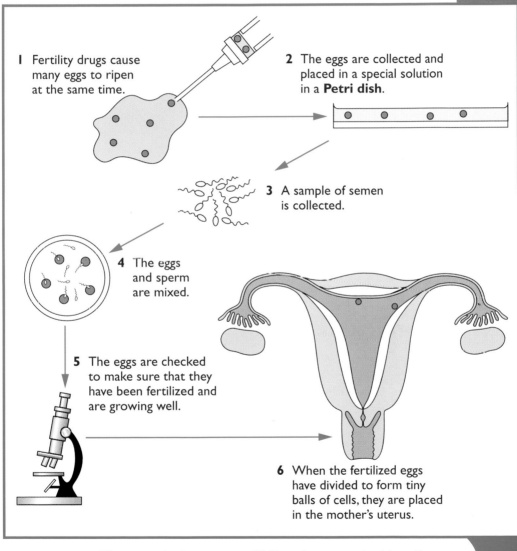

1 Fertility drugs cause many eggs to ripen at the same time.

2 The eggs are collected and placed in a special solution in a **Petri dish**.

3 A sample of semen is collected.

4 The eggs and sperm are mixed.

5 The eggs are checked to make sure that they have been fertilized and are growing well.

6 When the fertilized eggs have divided to form tiny balls of cells, they are placed in the mother's uterus.

The stages in the process of IVF can be summarized in a diagram like this. It makes it all look simple. Yet ,the technology used here has taken years to perfect, and it is still a long way from guaranteeing that a successful pregnancy will result.

The Price of Success

IVF is a technique that has improved the chances of having a baby for **infertile** couples all over the world. Thousands and thousands of children have been born as a result of this still relatively new technology. From an early success rate of well below 5 percent, couples now have a 20–25 percent chance of pregnancy when they undergo IVF. This success rate may sound low, but it is similar to the chances of a **fertile** couple getting pregnant if they have sexual intercourse at the fertile time of the month. In addition, the rate varies according to the infertility problem and the age of the woman.

These are just some of the tens of thousands of children who would not have been born without the technique of IVF.

A clinic lottery?

The chances of success vary greatly from clinic to clinic. Some clinics appear far better at producing live babies as a result of a single treatment than others. When people (or their health insurance companies) are spending large sums of money on treatments for infertility, they have a right to know that they are getting good value for their money. Yet the figures for babies born per treatment can be misleading and people need to look carefully before making judgments or choosing a clinic.

For example, some clinics treat a larger number of patients with difficult problems than others. Some clinics specialize in the treatment of older women or in using **donor** eggs, for which the chances of success are lower than for other IVF treatments. Another important factor affecting success rates is the number of **embryos** transferred into the body of the woman, which varies from clinic to clinic. The more embryos that are transferred, the greater the chance of multiple pregnancies. Multiple pregnancies, such as twins, triplets, or more, are known to increase the risk of things going wrong. Triplets and even higher numbers of babies put a huge strain on the mother's body when she is carrying them. They are also very difficult for parents to cope with when they are born. The physical and emotional demands of giving birth to and raising several children can be very hard to meet without lots of extra support. Yet if one or more of the embryos that has been implanted does not grow to form a baby some parents grieve for the potential babies they have lost.

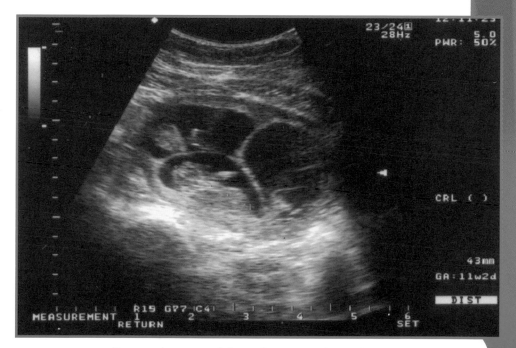

If more than one of the embryos transferred back to the mother's body implants successfully, then a multiple pregnancy results. After no babies at all, triplets (shown here) might sound exciting at first, but the reality can be very tough.

The scan showed twins ... I must admit I felt sad for my other little embryo and wondered where he had gone.
IVF mother who had three embryos transferred and gave birth to twins

If three or more babies arrive at once, a couple has to buy food, clothing, and everything else for a large family. So if the number of **embryos** transferred is not carefully managed, the longed-for arrival of children to an **infertile** couple can put a huge strain on them, particularly if they have spent a good part of their savings on infertility treatment. However, if clinics transferred only one embryo to reduce the risk of a multiple pregnancy, they would also reduce the likelihood of pregnancy. **Pros and cons** such as these need to be weighed carefully when couples and their doctors are deciding on treatment. In the U.S., a clinic typically implants two or three embryos at a time, to strike a balance between giving a good chance of pregnancy with the least risk of a large multiple birth. Clinics often decide on how many embryos to implant on an individual basis, taking into account factors such as a woman's health and age. In Britain, under the regulations of the Human Fertilisation and Embryology Authority (HFEA), three is the maximum number of embryos that can be transplanted at one time.

A frozen harvest

The number of embryos to implant is not the only dilemma facing IVF specialists and their patients. The production of more embryos than are needed for any one transfer means there are other **ethical** questions to be answered.

When the **ovaries** are encouraged to **superovulate,** they can produce twelve or more mature eggs in one **menstrual cycle**. These eggs are **fertilized,** and several healthy embryos are then transferred back into the **uterus** of the mother. But this leaves a problem. There may well be other healthy embryos remaining in their dishes. What is to be done with these other embryos?

The use of frozen human **sperm** goes back many years. The use of frozen human embryos is much more recent, although animal embryos have been transported around the world in this way for some time. Freezing seems a very dramatic treatment for such delicate tissue, but it appears to cause no damage. Here, frozen embryos are being removed from storage.

Most IVF clinics offer embryo freezing and storage to their clients. The early embryos are frozen and stored in containers of liquid nitrogen. This has many advantages. If the first attempt at IVF fails, the couple can have at least one if not more attempts without having to go through the whole process of **fertility drugs** and egg collection again. If, on the other hand, the first attempt is successful, then the remaining embryos can be kept so that, if and when the couple decides they would like another child, they have embryos ready to use. Again this makes the whole process quicker, less traumatic, and less expensive for all concerned. However, the presence of these frozen embryos does raise some questions. One of the simplest is What happens to the embryos once a couple decides their family is complete?

The embryos may simply be destroyed, but this is not the most usual fate for them. Often a couple may donate their "spare" embryos to another infertile couple who cannot produce healthy ones. Many other couples decide to keep their frozen embryos "just in case." But many clinics have embryos that have been in storage for ten years or more, and no one knows for sure the effect of long-term freezing on the health of the children who might grow from the embryos. Some couples may also choose to donate the embryos for further research into the treatment of human infertility. Because of the ethical issues surrounding research on human embryos in the U.S., the research must be privately funded, that is, not paid for with the money U.S. citizens pay as taxes. Many other countries also have laws limiting research that may be carried out on human embryos.

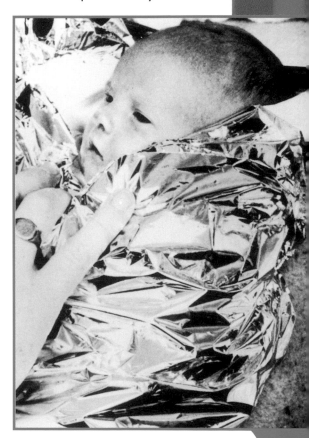

Zoe Leyland was born in Australia in 1984. She was the first frozen embryo to become a live baby, and seemed to suffer no ill effects from from her time in the deep freeze.

Doriver's Story

The theory of the causes of **infertility** and the way infertility can be overcome, including high-tech treatments like IVF, make the whole process sound very neat, orderly, and scientific. However, infertility involves real people and the treatments are not always straightforward. They can take a long time, and they often don't even work. So what is infertility treatment *really* like?

Doriver and Ian Lilley got married when Doriver was only 20. They planned to start a family about five years later. "In fact it was almost six years before I threw away my [birth control] pills. We were going on holiday and I half-expected to come back pregnant!" explained Doriver. But Doriver wasn't pregnant when they came back from their vacation, and she still wasn't pregnant eighteen months later. At this point Ian and Doriver went to see their doctor, but even at this stage they weren't too worried. They weren't in a huge hurry to have a family, it was just something that everybody did.

When Ian and Doriver Lilley got married in 1985, they expected to spend a few years saving up money before settling down to family life. But things didn't quite work out as planned.

Because they had already been trying for a baby for some time, and they had a sympathetic doctor, they were referred quite quickly to an infertility specialist. This isn't always the case. Some couples wait a very long time before they are referred to a specialist. As the tests got under way it all began to seem more serious. None of the initial tests showed any reason why Doriver and Ian were not getting pregnant. Yet nothing they tried worked. Even when the doctor suggested that they try the **fertility drug** clomiphene citrate, nothing happened. All of the treatments that had sounded so effective in theory did not have the desired effect on the reproductive systems of Doriver and Ian Lilley.

Every time something fails, infertility becomes harder to deal with, as you begin to realize it might not work—ever.

Doriver Lilley

Infertility takes over

The infertility began to take over Doriver's life. Soon she could think of little else. Ian, too, was unhappy: "The hardest part was watching the woman I love suffer so much pain and being unable to do anything about it."

For both of them, not feeling in control of the situation was a strange and very unpleasant experience. In most areas of life people have at least some level of control over their actions and choices. When infertility strikes, that control is removed. Not conceiving made Doriver feel like a failure. It was very hard to rely on other people for such a personal thing as having a baby. And so far, science had failed them, too.

Because Doriver and Ian live in Britain, their treatment up to this point was provided free by the government-funded National Health Service (NHS). For several years they tried a wide variety of treatments, but they did not conceive a baby, and doctors could not discover a clear reason for their infertility. The Lilleys were told they could not continue getting free infertility treatments. If they wanted to try IVF, they would have to pay for it themselves, because their NHS doctors felt there was little chance they would become pregnant.

Everyone else seemed pregnant. I kept going in to work, but it was so hard to keep appearing cheerful. Every day when I got home, I'd break down and cry because I couldn't cope with it….

Doriver Lilley

Beginning IVF

Making the decision to begin IVF treatment had a strange effect on Doriver and Ian. It made them feel a little better. The fact that they were trying something different, something very advanced and cutting-edge, gave them a renewed sense of optimism. Surely something was going to happen now! Again, in theory, IVF should be an uncomplicated solution, but where living systems are concerned, science and technology do not always cooperate.

Will IVF be the answer?

Their IVF treatment moved forward rapidly under the supervision of Dr. John Webster. Dr. Webster had been present at the birth of Louise Brown, the first test-tube baby, so Doriver and Ian felt they were in very good hands. However, they knew that if IVF didn't work, there was nothing else left to try. The first treatment was exciting. Doriver's eggs were harvested, which was in itself an exciting victory. Some healthy **embryos** developed and were transferred back into her body. Doriver and Ian even had a very weakly positive pregnancy test. However, the embryos did not implant properly, the levels of pregnancy **hormones** dropped, and the "pregnancy" ended just a few days later. In spite of the disappointment, Doriver was encouraged because eggs had been successfully harvested and embryos had formed.

The second attempt, however, was a crushing blow. It failed completely. The quality of the embryos was poor. Ideally, the cells making up an embryo are all the same size and have smooth **membranes**. The two that were transferred back into Doriver consisted of only two cells each. In addition, they had rough membranes with pieces breaking off. There was no pregnancy. Things looked bad. Financially the treatment had left them £6,000 (about $9,800) poorer, and they still didn't have a baby. Statistics show that a couple's chances of a successful pregnancy drop with each failed IVF treatment. And Doriver and Ian were well aware of these figures.

> *I knew that statistically our chances were getting less and less each time we tried—but I also knew that as long as we had any money to spend I was going to keep on trying.*
>
> Doriver Lilley

When Doriver and Ian came into a small amount of money, they immediately made an appointment for their third attempt at IVF.

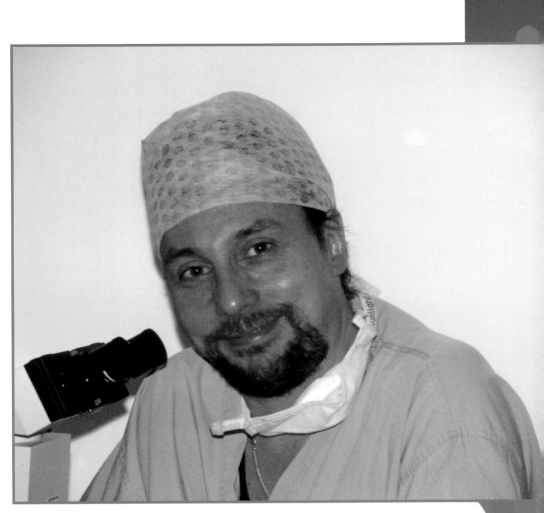

Steve Green is an **embryologist**, one of the team at the CARE clinic at The Park Hospital where Ian and Doriver went for treatment. His role was to make sure that the embryos that were replaced in Doriver's uterus were healthy and growing well.

*There was a huge pressure to provide good quality **sperm**. Doriver had been through so much, everything was ready and waiting . . .*

Ian Lilley

Eggs were harvested, healthy embryos formed, and were transferred into Doriver's **uterus**. Then the waiting began. This time the pregnancy test was strongly positive. At least one embryo had definitely implanted in the uterus wall!

Pregnant at last!

At age 32, after six years of trying, Doriver was finally pregnant. She couldn't believe it! She actually refused to accept that she really could be pregnant, yet was terrified in case anything went wrong with the pregnancy. She found herself constantly worried that she might miscarry (lose the baby during the pregnancy), but another six weeks passed with no problems.

> *After embryo replacement I did everything in the house [for Doriver] and got all our meals ready etc. I know that you are told it doesn't make any difference [what the woman does in her daily life], but after so long we were not going to take that chance.*
>
> Ian Lilley

Still refusing to believe what was happening, Doriver and Ian went for their first **ultrasound** scan. When it showed not one but two tiny beating hearts, two little **embryos** growing strongly, they were completely bowled over. Not only were they pregnant, they were expecting twins! By the time Daniel and Jordanne arrived safely, Doriver had only just accepted that she was pregnant. Nevertheless, she was still deeply anxious that things would go wrong.

> *Even when I was in labor, when I went into hospital, I kept thinking "This is it, this is when I'm going to lose them." I just couldn't believe we were really going to have children of our own.*
>
> Doriver Lilley

> *When I saw my son being born and I could see his face start to emerge I couldn't believe I was finally to meet my children after so long.*
>
> Ian Lilley

After the twins were born, Doriver had little time to marvel at how they had arrived. Caring for newborn twins is enormously time-consuming and tiring. But this was what all the trying and waiting had been about. During **infertility** treatment the focus is on getting pregnant. It can be easy to forget that at the end of a pregnancy there are babies that grow up into children that must be cared for.

However, fate had one more twist in store for Doriver and Ian. Just when Doriver was planning to return to work, she found she was pregnant again, without any artificial intervention. Doriver and Ian were shocked. Once again, the unpredictability of human **fertility** had thrown their plans into disarray. Science had been unable to explain their infertility, even though it had eventually helped them to overcome it. Now science could not really explain their new-found fertility. But once they had got over the shock, there was excitement all around when baby James made his entry into the world. Doriver and Ian are now the happy, proud, exhausted, and somewhat bewildered parents of three lovely, healthy children—Daniel, Jordanne, and James. They are also a glowing advertisement for what IVF can achieve. The years of research that went into the development of IVF technology have brought happy endings like this for thousands and thousands of couples around the world.

Doriver with Daniel, Jordanne, and their little brother James. As these children grow up, there will be no way of telling that two of them would not exist if it weren't for IVF technology.

Beyond IVF

The techniques of IVF are constantly being refined and adjusted to find ways of giving the highest possible chance of success to **infertile** couples. For example, for many years **embryos** have been transferred at the four- or eight-cell stage. Recent work suggests that transferring the **blastocysts** (five-day-old embryos) will give better pregnancy rates, because this is the stage at which the embryo would enter the **uterus** in a natural **conception**.

However, there have also been a number of other new technologies developed that help overcome even more **fertility** problems. Most of these also involve embryo transfer.

Donor eggs

One of the ways in which IVF has moved forward is in the use of **donor** eggs. It has been shown that if a couple is having trouble conceiving and the woman is over 40, it may be necessary to use an egg donor to achieve a successful pregnancy. In couples with this problem, IVF has been shown to be much more successful when the eggs of a woman who is less than 37 years old and who is already known to be fertile are used. However, it is not just in couples where the woman is older that donor eggs are very useful. Women who have no eggs in their **ovaries** cannot become pregnant without an egg donor. Also, women who carry a **genetic** disease may want to use donor eggs to avoid passing on a serious illness to her children. The use of donor eggs in IVF, along with donor embryos mentioned earlier, has increased the success rate for older women.

> Fertility in women is known to decline with age, strikingly so after 35, and reproductive capacity is all but lost by the age of 45.
>
> Andrew Kan and Hossam Abdulla,
> IVF specialists, Lister Hospital

Some doctors use this technology to allow women who are well over the natural age for childbearing to have children. Naturally, a woman passes through the menopause at between 45 and 55 years. At this point she no longer has **periods** and her ovaries became inactive. No more eggs are released. But by using donor eggs or embryos, women over the age of 50 have been able to give birth.

In 1994, Rosanna della Corte, an Italian woman, gave birth to a baby boy when she was 62. Artificial **hormones** had been used to prepare her uterus, and once the pregnancy was established her body took over and maintained the pregnancy just like that of a younger woman.

Since the first breakthrough, more than 100 women age 50 or over have had babies in the United States alone. However, not many infertility clinics will agree to carry out this treatment for older women. There are many people who have concerns about it, both because of the potential risks to the health of the mother and the age gap between the mother and child—although similar arguments are rarely put forward when older men father children naturally!

When that child is of college age, his mother will be 80. That is, if she is still alive. We're designing orphans by choice, and we say this is OK?
John Paris, professor of **bioethics** at Boston College
and a Jesuit priest, speaking of Rosanna della Corte's offspring

GIFT—another alternative

GIFT stands for Gamete Intra Fallopian Transfer. It is a modified version of IVF that involves harvesting the eggs and placing them and the **sperm** into a healthy **fallopian tube**. The idea is that **fertilization** then takes place within the natural environment of the body instead of in a glass dish, and any **embryos** that form will then travel down the remaining part of the fallopian tube to the **uterus** where they will implant as normal. GIFT has a success rate similar to that of IVF. However, because it involves surgery (a **laparoscopy**) most clinics prefer to use IVF.

Injecting sperm—a major breakthrough

Until recently there was no help for couples in which the male partner did not produce fertile sperm, apart from **artificial insemination** by a **donor**. Recent developments have changed all that. There are now techniques available that mean it is possible, in theory at least, for almost any man to father a child.

The main technique used is known as **ICSI**. This stands for Intra Cytoplasmic Sperm Injection. Eggs are harvested from a woman after treatment with **fertility drugs** in the same way as for IVF. A single sperm is then injected into the **cytoplasm** of each egg cell. The fertilized eggs are then observed as they divide to form early embryos.

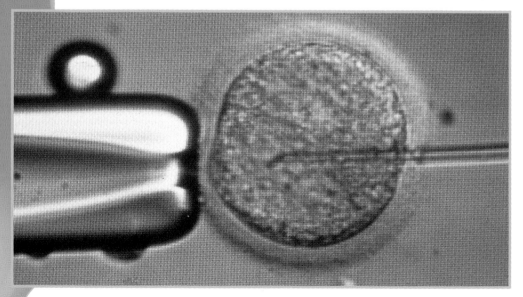

ICSI involves using a needle to inject a single sperm directly into an egg so that fertilization can take place. The sperm doesn't have to break down the outer layers of the egg.

Two or three healthy embryos will then be returned to the body of the mother just as in normal IVF treatment.

> *ICSI technology has revolutionized the treatment of male factor infertility. This is considerable, because we now appreciate that male factor infertility is probably the single largest cause of infertility amongst couples.*
>
> Dr. Simon Fischel, CARE clinic, The Park Hospital

ICSI was developed by researchers in Belgium. The first baby to be born using ICSI was born in 1992. By the late 1990s, ICSI was a well-established procedure in infertility clinics in the U.S., Europe, and Australia. By 2001, more than a thousand babies worldwide had been born using ICSI. In fact ICSI is now chosen as the best treatment for at least 30 percent of couples who need IVF technology.

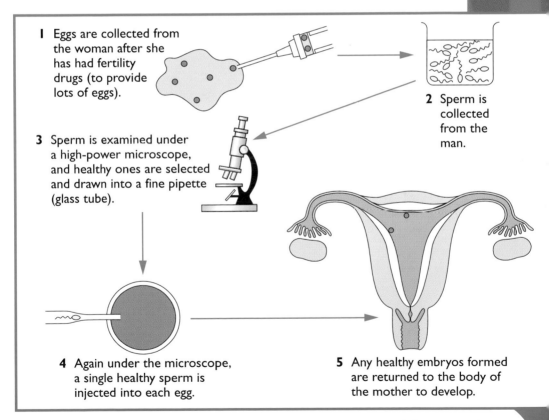

1 Eggs are collected from the woman after she has had fertility drugs (to provide lots of eggs).

2 Sperm is collected from the man.

3 Sperm is examined under a high-power microscope, and healthy ones are selected and drawn into a fine pipette (glass tube).

4 Again under the microscope, a single healthy sperm is injected into each egg.

5 Any healthy embryos formed are returned to the body of the mother to develop.

The ICSI procedure benefits two groups of patients: One group it can help is men who have very few healthy sperm or who cannot produce **semen** at all, because with ICSI only one sperm is needed to fertilize an egg. A second group that benefits is couples who produce healthy eggs and sperm for IVF but cannot achieve fertilization. ICSI can solve the problem with the direct insertion of a sperm into an egg.

45

Ethics, Issues, and the Law

The new reproductive technologies, including IVF and other procedures, have brought great happiness to thousands of couples who have been enabled to have children. In the United States alone more than 45,000 children have been born as a result of IVF. However, IVF technologies have also raised many issues that people need to consider. Some of the issues are very practical and are the direct result of IVF technology.

> When making decisions about **infertility** treatment you have to consider the MEEF equation:
> Medical issues + Ethical issues + Emotional issues + Financial issues = Treatment.
>> Michael Dooley, consultant,
>> Winterbourne Hospital Infertility Clinic

Money matters

One important issue is that of cost. IVF treatment is expensive. In the U.S., many health care plans will pay only for limited infertility treatments, which may exclude IVF. Some will not cover any type of infertility treatment at all. Although some states require health plans to cover infertility treatments, many large companies that have their own private health insurance plans do not have to follow these rulings. Some individuals have challenged their health insurance company's refusal to cover infertility treatments in court with some success. Still, many infertile couples in the U.S. end up paying for treatment out of their own pockets. In both Britain and Australia the government-funded national health plans pay for a certain amount of infertility treatment. However, there are questions about whether it is right for large amounts of state money to be used to help infertile couples have children, when there is a shortage of money for medical treatments for diseases that can be life threatening.

Frozen embryos

If a treatment cycle results in more healthy **embryos** than can be safely transferred into the woman, then those embryos are often frozen for possible later use. If the parents of those embryos later divorce, who do the embryos belong to? This is an important issue because ultimately the parents of the embryos decide what will happen to them. If the couple gets divorced and does not agree about the fate of the embryos, who then takes responsibility for them? Another scenario that must be considered is that of both parents dying in an accident before they have successfully had children. If there are still healthy frozen embryos, should they be implanted inside a **surrogate mother** and brought into the world to inherit their parents' belongings?

In all of these debates the welfare of the potential children is the most important issue. It could be extremely damaging for children to feel that they had been pawns in their parents' divorce settlement or brought into being to make sure money stayed in the family.

In theory, frozen embryos could be preserved for about 10,000 years before the natural background radiation of the Earth damaged their **DNA** to the extent that they would not grow and develop properly. In practice, after a certain amount of time most couples decide either to implant the embryos themselves, donate them to another couple, or allow them to be used for research.

In Britain there are legal limits. Frozen embryos can only be kept for five years, with another five years' extension possible if the parents need more time to make a decision. This gives a total of ten years of embryo storage. As no one knows for sure how long frozen embryos can be stored safely, this limit attempts to protect children who might be born damaged in some way from eggs stored for longer than ten years. The U.S. does not have specific limits for the length of time frozen embryos may be stored, although some clinics have their own limits and recommendations. This raises child welfare issues, making it possible, in theory, for one sibling to be decades younger than the other.

Initially the embryos just offered me an option, another chance of having a baby, but we'd lost so many embryos they didn't really mean a lot. But once I'd had Daniel and Jordanne, part of me had a sentimental vision of these tiny babies frozen. I had given the twins their chance of life, shouldn't I do the same for the frozen embryos? And then the logical part of me says that they are collections of four cells, and that it would be better to give them to someone else or let them be used for research. It's really difficult....

Doriver Lilley

47

Embryo research

The use of **embryos** for research is another very sensitive issue. Without embryo research, **infertility** treatment would never have reached the point it has today. Yet this research is carried out on tiny clusters of cells, some of which might, if transferred into a woman's body, turn into babies. For some people this is very difficult to accept. There are groups of people in every country in which this type of research is carried out who object to it very strongly. For this reason, the U.S. does not allow federal funds to be used for research carried out on human embryos.

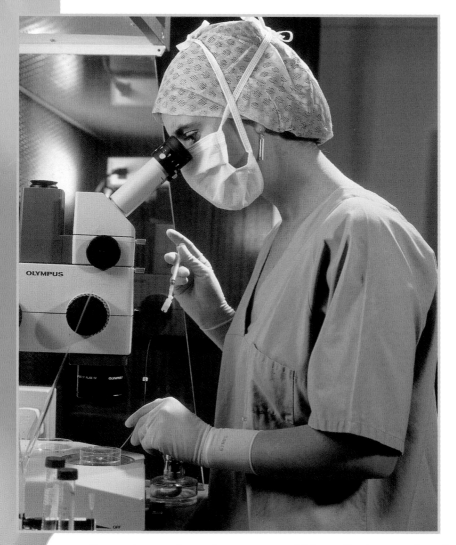

Research on embryos is a controversial issue. But in countries where it is legal the research will continue, and infertile couples and couples with **genetic** diseases will benefit from the results.

Surrogate mothers

The ability to **fertilize** eggs outside of the body has paved the way for another controversial form of infertility treatment—the use of a **surrogate mother.** Some women have **ovaries** that work perfectly well but they do not have a **uterus**, while other women have no reproductive organs at all. Their only chance of having a baby, apart from adoption, is if another woman will carry a baby for them. This might involve IVF, with embryos from one couple transferred into the uterus of another woman or it might involve **artificial insemination** of the surrogate mother with **sperm** from the father. Whatever the method, the baby grows and develops inside the surrogate mother, who then hands the baby over to the parents very shortly after birth.

There are problems with surrogacy. In the U.S., it is legal and is carried out for money by a number of very successful businesses. In Britain and Australia, it is legal but there can be no payment given to a woman for carrying another person's child. The biggest problem that may occur is that the surrogate mother may decide she cannot hand over the child. There have been legal battles between biological and surrogate parents. In the first test case in the U.S., the "purchasing" parents were granted custody of the child, but the surrogate mother was allowed visiting rights.

There have been a number of successful surrogate mother relationships, including ones in which a sister has carried a baby for her sister who is unable to have children, as shown here. Many surrogate mothers already have their own children and feel they are giving the gift of a child to someone else.

49

The law

With the arrival of new technologies there have been legal issues. When dealing with potential human life the risks are great. Different countries have decided to deal with them in different ways. The first concern in most legislation is the welfare of any potential children born using the new technologies. If there is concern that the health or well-being of the babies conceived might be affected by the technology, then most countries have serious objections about its use.

IVF began in Britain, and Britain responded to this giant step forward with a regulatory body known as the Human Fertilisation and Embryology Authority, or HFEA. Set up in 1991, the HFEA makes sure that all clinics offering IVF and other **infertility** treatments in Britain meet strict standards. They collect information about success rates, and provide information to the public. The HFEA also licenses and monitors

When people wish to change the law they often stage a protest, like these people here. Attempts to change national law in Australia to allow states to ban IVF for single people sparked off such protests.

all **embryo** research, supervises what is going on, and balances what should and should not be done. Decisions are made by the 21 members of the HFEA, who are experts in relevant fields. To make sure that a wide variety of views are heard, more than half of the members are not involved in medicine or human embryo research.

*The first IVF baby was born in the U.K. [Britain] and we were the first **statutory** government body to regulate this treatment and remain one of the few to do so. While the number of couples seeking IVF treatment rapidly increases we aim to assure a high standard of care and medical expertise whether that clinic is private or public, big or small.*

Ruth Deech, HFEA chairman

So, in Britain, the regulations regarding infertility treatments are relatively straightforward. If a treatment is allowed by the HFEA it goes ahead, if it is not it doesn't.

In other countries things are not so clear-cut. In the U.S. there are few laws controlling what techniques or research may or may not be carried out. However, in most U.S. clinics, doctors and technicians work to the same high scientific, medical, and ethical standards expected from infertility clinic staff all around the world. In fact, the American Society for Reproductive Medicine (ASRM), an organization representing the nation's fertility doctors, issues a set of guidelines and standards for maintaining a safe, professional, and successful clinic. Among the issues addressed by the ASRM are educational and training requirements for clinic staff and quality-assurance standards for the clinic laboratories. A majority of U.S. clinics follow these guidelines and standards and report data regarding their activities and success rates to a branch of the ASRM, the Society for Assisted Reproductive Technologies (SART). SART then makes the information available to the public.

In Australia the fact that there are two layers of legislation, national legislation and legislation at the state level, has caused problems and confusion. For example, in Australia one state wanted to prevent single people from receiving IVF treatment. Many people protested this. In response to the outcry, national law was used to stop the state law. There have since been moves to try and change the national law to allow states to make their own decisions. A solution has yet to be found.

A matter of faith

The decisions a couple makes about **infertility** treatments may be affected by their religious beliefs. There is no single view within the different faiths about the acceptability of infertility treatments such as IVF. This means that one couple may undergo IVF sure in the belief that it is acceptable, while another couple, equally desperate to have a child, may feel unable to accept IVF.

Below are summaries of the official views of some major religions, regarding infertility treatments and related issues. It is important to remember, however, that many people who consider themselves followers of a certain religion may not necessarily agree with the strict, official view handed down by their faith's leaders. In fact, within some faiths there may be disagreement among religious leaders about what is and is not acceptable. In addition to religious beliefs, couples often need to think about the effect infertility is having on their mental and physical health and seek medical as well as religious advice before making a decision.

The Roman Catholic standpoint

The teaching of the Roman Catholic Church on infertility treatments is strict and is the same in every country. In 1987 the Pope made the Catholic position very clear in a document called *Donum vitae* ("Respect for Life"). He said that treatments such as IVF are not acceptable because they separate the **conception** of a child from the sexual act between the parents. The Roman Catholic Church also rejects completely any infertility treatment that involves donated eggs, **sperm,** or **embryos** as gravely immoral because of the introduction of another person into the marriage bond.

A Muslim perspective

Within Islam the bearing of children is a vitally important part of married life. In addition, Islamic teaching states that for every illness there is a cure, so it is regarded as acceptable and correct that an infertile couple should seek help. Treatments such as **fertility drugs** and procedures to open up the **fallopian tubes** are fully acceptable treatments for Muslims to undergo. Islamic scholars also accept the use of IVF. However, they make it clear that IVF is acceptable only if enormous care is taken that only the eggs and sperm of the husband and wife concerned are used in the treatment. As in many other religions, the use of donated eggs, donated sperm, or donated embryos is viewed as completely unacceptable because it breaks the unity of the marriage bond.

For many people the spiritual dimension of their lives—their religion—is important in guiding their decisions about infertility treatments.

The Jewish approach

As in so many other religions, the family is very important to the Jewish faith. The three main branches of Judaism, Orthodox, Conservative, and Reform, all have differing views on the acceptability of IVF technologies. Orthodox Jewish law finds assisted **reproduction** acceptable in helping a Jewish couple to conceive a child as long as the eggs and sperm come from the parents themselves. Therefore, IVF using sex cells from the parents is acceptable, and there is often a **rabbinical** supervisor present to make sure that the eggs and sperm are not contaminated by material from non-Jews. But the use of **donor** eggs or sperm is much less acceptable, and certainly not allowed if the sex cells are not from Jewish people. Conservative and Reform leaders also accept IVF using the sex cells of the parents. In addition, the Reform branch allows **artificial insemination** using donor sperm or IVF using donor eggs. Many Conservative leaders will also permit these practices, but only as a last resort.

The Hindu approach

For Hindus, with their beliefs in reincarnation and caste (inherited social status), treatments such as IVF raise many problems. Only a husband is allowed to touch his wife, so a doctor cannot intervene in the act of conception, and fear of caste contamination makes donor eggs and sperm unacceptable to strict Hindus.

Where Do We Go from Here?

One of the most exciting developments in IVF technology is the ability to help avoid **genetic** diseases. In some families there are errors in the genetic code that result in incurable diseases that can be fatal. In Tay Sachs disease, which mainly affects Jewish families, the nervous system of the child gradually breaks down. The child dies before reaching five years of age. Huntington's disease affects people in their 40s or 50s, causing permanent damage to the brain followed by death. Another disease, cystic fibrosis, causes the cells of all the tubes in the body to produce a thick, sticky **mucus** that blocks the tubes and allows massive infections to build up. It shortens life expectancy considerably.

Down's syndrome is one of many inherited genetic disorders. For some families with these conditions, genetic screening and IVF offer ways of ensuring that their children are free from the disease. However, some couples feel they cannot use these methods because it is against their faith.

For couples who know that they may carry these diseases, the decision to have a family is not an easy one because it involves a genetic lottery. While all their children may be born healthy, if they are very unlucky they will all suffer from the genetic disease. However, IVF technology combined with methods developed for **genetic engineering** offers some hope. In some specialized clinics, couples carrying genetic diseases can be helped to have healthy children. Some genetic diseases such as hemophilia (in which the blood does not clot properly) and Duchenne muscular dystrophy (in which the muscles deteriorate until the child dies) only affect boys. These diseases are known as sex-linked diseases. If a couple plans to have a baby using IVF, a single cell from each developing **embryo** can be extracted and its sex determined. Girls have two X **chromosomes** in the **nucleus** of their cells, while boys have an X and a Y. When there is a risk of sex-linked disease, only female embryos will be transferred to the mother, so a daughter free from the genetic disease is guaranteed.

Recently, scientists have obtained a much better understanding of the whole of the human genetic material (known as the human genome) including many individual genes. As a result it is becoming increasingly possible to identify embryos that carry disease-causing genes.

In a complex procedure that currently takes place only at a few clinics, one cell is removed from the embryo. Using technology developed for genetic engineering, the **DNA** from the cell is duplicated many times over. With such a large sample, individual faulty genes can be picked out by comparing them with known DNA profiles using the comparison technique shown above. Only healthy embryos are then transferred to the mother's body.

Cloning

Cloning mammals involves making an identical copy of an adult animal. This has been done a number of times with animals such as sheep.

Dolly the sheep was cloned from the adult cell of another sheep. The **nucleus** of an adult cell was placed in an egg cell and then transferred to the **uterus** of the **surrogate mother**. Scientists are still investigating Dolly. So far, despite some signs of early aging, she has given birth naturally to a lamb of her own.

In late 2001, scientists working for a privately funded U.S. biotechnology company transferred adult human **DNA** into an unfertilized human egg cell. The egg divided until it reached the six-cell stage. Even though the experiment's purpose was to create embryonic **stem cells** for potential use in treating diseases and not for reproductive purposes, the feat created a stir. Many people feared that the cloning of humans might not be far off. IVF could make it possible. A cloned **embryo** could be implanted in a **uterus** to grow and develop into a baby. In many nations this is illegal, but some scientists are still planning to try and produce the first human clone. They feel it could solve **infertility**. If an infertile woman could give birth to a clone of her partner or herself, there would be no need to use **donor sperm** or eggs, which can be in short supply and raise religious objections.

Into the future

The future of infertility treatments looks bright. The techniques are being improved all the time, and the numbers of people who have a child through IVF or related treatments continue to grow. Hundreds of thousands of IVF babies are alive today, who would not exist without the groundbreaking scientific techniques that allow eggs to be **fertilized** outside of their mother's body. The benefits to the individuals concerned are immeasurable and society also benefits from the birth of more children free from **genetic** diseases.

However, there are two sides to every story. Many people question the acceptability of some of the treatments now being suggested, such as cloning and the use of spare embryos for the development of medical treatments. But the clock cannot be turned back. We cannot return to the situation before these treatments were discovered. And for many infertile couples, IVF technologies have brought much happiness. The development of IVF and other treatments will continue for the foreseeable future, fulfilling an ever-growing demand, and the debate within society will continue alongside it.

Louise Brown, the very first test-tube baby, is now a young woman. Here she holds two of the hundreds of thousands of IVF babies that have joined her since those early, groundbreaking days in 1978!

Timeline

200   Records show Jewish thinkers discussed the possibility of accidental or unintentional **artificial insemination**.

1300s   Accounts exist of Arabs using artificial insemination on horses.

1777   Italian priest begins experiments with the artificial insemination of reptiles.

1785   First attempts at human artificial insemination by John Hunter, a Scottish surgeon. A baby is born the same year as a result.

1890   In Britain, Robert Dickinson begins experimenting with **donor sperm**, although his work is carried out in secret because of religious opposition.

1945   Early reports of artificial insemination using donor sperm published in the *British Medical Journal*.

1949   Dr. Piero Donini, an Italian, produces the first human **fertility drug**.

1954   Four successful pregnancies take place using previously frozen sperm.

1960s   Major breakthroughs increase understanding of the female reproductive system and the process of **fertilization**. Drugs are developed that stimulate **ovaries** so they produce eggs, and **laparoscopy** methods are improved, making the treatment safer.

1962   First baby born as a result of drug-triggered **ovulation**.

1969   Human **in vitro fertilization** is achieved for the first time.

1975 First IVF pregnancy occurs, but it is an **ectopic pregnancy**.

1978 Birth of Louise Brown, the first "test-tube" baby born as a result of IVF.

1980 Two Australian teams succeed in IVF deliveries after drug-induced **superovulation** in the mother.

1984 The Warnock Report in Britain calls for a **statutory** body to control reproductive technology.

1988–9 **GIFT** introduced and the first successful pregnancies achieved.

1990 Human Fertilisation and Embryology Act passes in Britain followed by the setting up of the Human Fertilisation and Embryology Authority (HFEA) in 1991.

1992 First baby born as a result of **ICSI**.

1994 At the age of 62, Rosanna della Corte gives birth to a son after IVF treatment.

1996 The birth of Dolly the sheep, the first cloned mammal.

1998 Growing embryonic **stem cells** in the laboratory opens the way for different types of cells and organs to be grown as needed for use in transplant surgery. Some of these stem cells come from "spare" embryos donated by couples who had successful IVF treatment.

2001 Teams in the U.S. and Italy make the controversial announcement that they are working on producing the first human clone in order offer **infertile** couples another way of having children.

Glossary

artificial insemination inserting **sperm** into the vagina using a device, rather than through sexual intercourse

bioethics the moral rights and wrongs of situations linked to biological advances

blastocyst hollow ball of cells formed after the **fertilization** of an egg

cervix lower part of the **uterus** that extends into the vagina

chromosome one of the threadlike structures in a **nucleus**, made up of **DNA** and protein. Each chromosome carries many different genes.

circumvent to get around something

conception **fertilization** of an egg by a **sperm**, followed by the egg's implantation in the wall of the uterus

contraception using a condom, birth-control pill, or other method to prevent pregnancy

cytoplasm jellylike substance that fills the cell and in which the components of the cell are suspended

DNA (deoxyribonucleic acid) type of nucleic acid, found in the **nucleus** of a cell, which carries the **genetic** code

donor someone who gives an organ or a product of their body, such as eggs or **sperm**, to help someone who has a faulty organ or product

ectopic pregnancy pregnancy in which the embryo implants and develops in one of the **fallopian tubes** instead of in the **uterus**

embryo term for an egg after it has been **fertilized,** when it is in its early stages of development

embryologist doctor or scientist who specializes in the study of **embryos**

enzyme special protein that makes possible or speeds up the rate of chemical reactions

estrogen female sex **hormone** made by the **ovaries,** involved in the release of a mature egg

ethics consideration of what is morally right or wrong

fallopian tube one of two tubes that links the **ovaries** and the **uterus** in the female reproductive system

fertility, fertile ability to produce offspring

fertility drugs chemicals that stimulate the development of mature eggs in the **follicles** of the **ovary**

fertilization union of egg and **sperm** that is necessary to produce offspring

follicle cell surrounding the developing egg in the **ovary**

Follicle Stimulating Hormone (FSH) sex **hormone** that causes some of the **follicles** of the **ovary** to ripen and the eggs within them to mature

genetic to do with the genes, the units of inheritance that are passed on from parent to offspring and determine the offspring's characteristics. Each gene is made from a length of **DNA**, found in the **nucleus** of a cell.

genetic engineering process by which the **genetic** material of a cell may be altered either by replacing damaged genetic material or by adding extra genetic material

GIFT Gamete Intra Fallopian Transfer, a modified version of IVF that involves harvesting the eggs and mixing them with **sperm** before replacing them inside the **fallopian tube**

gynecologist doctor who specializes in problems of the female reproductive system

hormone chemical messenger made in one place in the body that has an effect somewhere else in the body

ICSI an abbreviation of Intra Cytoplasmic Sperm Injection, the injection of a single **sperm** right into the **cytoplasm** of each egg cell

in vitro fertilization (IVF) term used to describe the **fertilization** of an egg in a glass **Petri dish**. In vitro is Latin for "in glass."

infertility, infertile inability to produce offspring

laparoscopy technique for looking at the **fallopian tube**s by inserting a medical instrument into the abdomen

membrane thin, skinlike tissue covering organs and cells

menstrual cycle approximately 28-day cycle of female **fertility**

mucus slimy substance produced by **membranes** in some parts of the body

nucleus (plural = nuclei) central part of a cell, which controls many cell functions and contains a person's **DNA**

ovaries two female sex organs where eggs are stored and where they mature and where **estrogen** and **progesterone** are produced

ovulation release of a mature egg from the **ovary**

ovum (egg) female sex cell

period time (usually lasting 5–7 days) during the **menstrual cycle** when pregnancy has not occurred and when the lining of the **uterus** is shed resulting in bleeding. Also called menstruation.

Petri dish small shallow dish made from thin glass, traditionally used for studying the behavior of bacteria

physiologist someone who studies the human body and its functions

pituitary gland small structure in the brain that produces many **hormones**

progesterone pregnancy **hormone** that prevents menstruation from occurring

pros and cons reasons for and against something

puberty stage when the body of a child undergoes physical development to become a sexually mature adult

rabbinical concerned with Jewish law

reproduction the making of a new individual

semen mixture of **sperm** and fluids produced by a man when he ejaculates (discharges semen)

sperm male sex cell

statutory having legal authority

stem cell "immortal" cell that retains the ability to divide and multiply and to create other types of cell. Stem cells are found in embryos, bone marrow, skin, intestine, and muscle tissue.

superovulation the production by a woman's body of many mature **follicles** containing mature eggs ready for release at the same time

surrogate mother woman who carries a baby for a couple who are unable to have a child of their own

testes pair of male sex organs in which **sperm** and **semen** are produced along with the male sex **hormone** testosterone

ultrasound refers to the use of extremely high-frequency sound waves to produce images of the inside of the human body. Used for examining developing babies in the **uterus**.

uterus organ of the female reproductive system in which the baby grows and develops (also known as the womb)

Further Reading

Avraham, Regina, *The Reproductive System,* Bromall, Penn.: Chelsea House Publishers, 2000.

Fullick, Ann. *Science Topics: The Human Body*, Des Plaines, Ill.: Heinemann Library, 1998.

Jackson, Donna M. *Twin Tales: The Magic and Mystery of Multiple Birth,* Boston: Little, Brown & Company, 2001.

Parker, Steve. *Reproduction and Growing Up,* Brookfield, Conn.: Millbrook Press, 1998.

Royston, Angela. *Birth and Reproduction,* Des Plaines, Ill.: Heinemann Library, 1997.

Index

American Society for Reproductive Medicine (ASRM) 51
artificial insemination 18, 19, 44, 49, 52

blastocysts 20, 21, 42
Brown, Louise 23, 39, 57

cervix 8, 14, 29
child welfare issues 47, 50
cloning 56, 57
conception 13, 16, 42, 52
contraception 5, 11
counseling 24

DNA 20, 47, 55
donor eggs 13, 33, 42–3, 52, 53, 56
donor embryos 35, 42, 52, 53
donor sperm 15, 19, 52, 53, 56
dye tests 14

ectopic pregnancy 22
Edwards, Dr. Robert 21, 22, 23, 24
eggs (ova) 4, 6, 7, 8, 9, 12–13, 16–17, 20, 21, 22, 24, 26-8
  donor eggs 13, 33, 42–43, 52, 53, 56
  harvesting 16, 21, 22, 27, 44, 45
embryos 5, 20, 22, 24, 28–29, 33–34, 39, 42, 44, 45, 55
  donor embryos 35, 42, 52, 53
  embryo research 35, 47, 48, 50, 57
  frozen embryos 34–35, 46–47
estrogen 7
ethics 5, 46–49

fallopian tubes 7, 8, 9, 13–14, 20, 22, 24, 44, 52, 53

fertility 6, 10, 11, 18, 42
fertility drugs 16, 17, 19, 20, 24, 26, 37, 45, 52
fertilization 4, 9, 13, 18, 20, 28, 34, 44, 49, 57
Follicle Stimulating Hormone (FSH) 7, 13, 16
follicles 21, 26, 27
funding infertility treatment 25, 37, 46, 51

genetic diseases 28, 42, 48, 54–5, 57
genetic engineering 55, 56
genetics 9, 20
GIFT (Gamete Intra Fallopian Transfer) 44

hormones 6–7, 13, 16, 19, 26, 27, 29, 39
Human Fertilisation and Embryology Authority (HFEA) 34, 50, 51
hysterosalpingogram 13, 14

ICSI (Intra Cytoplasmic Sperm Injection) 45, 46
implantation 9, 20, 29, 44
in vitro fertilization (IVF) 5, 11, 16, 18–35, 38–40, 46, 49, 50, 52, 53, 56
  background to 18–20
  case history 36–41
  embryo transfer 29, 42
  failed treatments 39
  first instance of 21
  process 24–25, 26–29, 31
  success rates 32
infertility 5, 10–15, 18, 37
infertility clinics 25, 32–33, 34, 50, 51

laparoscopy 14, 21, 22, 44
legal issues 47, 49, 50–51
lifestyle factors 10, 15, 16

menstrual cycle 6, 8, 26, 34
menstruation 7
multiple pregnancies 17, 24, 31, 33–34

new technologies 42–45

older women 33, 42–43
ovaries 6, 7, 12, 16, 19, 21, 26, 34, 42, 43, 49
ovulation 7, 8, 12, 13, 19, 22, 29

periods 30, 43
pituitary gland 6, 7, 19
pregnancy tests 30, 39
progesterone 29

religious issues 52–53
reproduction 6, 18, 20
semen 7, 8, 14–15, 28
sperm 4, 5, 7, 8, 9, 13, 14, 15, 24, 28, 39, 44
  donor sperm 15, 19, 52, 53, 56
  frozen sperm 19, 34
  injecting 5, 15, 44–45
  sperm count 15
Steptoe, Patrick 21, 22, 23, 24
superovulation 24, 34
surrogate mothers 47, 49, 56

test-tube babies 23
testes 7, 15, 19

ultrasound scans 26, 30, 40
Uniform Parentage Act 19
uterus 7, 8, 9, 13, 17, 20, 24, 29, 34, 42, 49, 56